EXPLORING COUNTRIES

INDIA

Tracy Vonder Brink

TABLE OF CONTENTS

A Crabtree Seedlings Book

Crabtree Publishing
crabtreebooks.com

School-to-Home Support for Caregivers and Teachers

This book helps children grow by letting them practice reading. Here are a few guiding questions to help the reader with building his or her comprehension skills. Possible answers appear here in red.

Before Reading:

- What do I think this book is about?
    - *I think this book is about India.*
    - *I think this book is about the food people eat in India.*
- What do I want to learn about this topic?
    - *I want to learn where India is.*
    - *I want to learn about the weather in India.*

During Reading:

- I wonder why…
    - *I wonder why the Taj Mahal is famous.*
    - *I wonder why dolphins live in the Ganges River.*
- What have I learned so far?
    - *I have learned that India is a peninsula.*
    - *I have learned that New Delhi is India's capital.*

After Reading:

- What details did I learn about this topic?
    - *I have learned that the Ganges River is India's longest river.*
    - *I have learned that Mumbai is India's biggest city.*
- Read the book again and look for the vocabulary words.
    - *I see the word* ***peninsula*** *on page 3, and the word* ***emperor*** *on page 8. The other glossary words are on pages 22 and 23.*

India is a country.

It is in South **Asia**.

India is a **peninsula**.

New Delhi is India's **capital**.

India has 22 official languages. Many people speak Hindi.

It is part of the **territory** of Delhi.

The Qutb Minar is in Delhi. It was built more than 800 years ago.

The Qutb Minar is a minaret, which is a kind of tower.

The Taj Mahal is a famous building.

It is in the city of Agra.

Long ago, an **emperor** built the Taj Mahal to remember his wife.

The Himalayas are mountains that stretch over part of India.

Some of the world's tallest mountains are in the Himalayas.

The Ganges River begins in the Himalayas.

It is the longest river in India.

Millions of people live along the Ganges.

Many animals live in the Ganges.

Gharial crocodiles swim in its waters.

So do Ganges river dolphins.

The Thar Desert is covered in sand dunes.

Camels live there.

The Western Ghats mountain range has **tropical** forests.

Bengal tigers make their homes there.

So do Asian elephants.

Mumbai is on the **coast**.

It is India’s biggest city.

India has amazing places to see!

More than 21 million people live in Mumbai.

Glossary

Asia (AY-zhuh): The continent between Europe and Africa on one side and the Pacific Ocean on the other

capital (KAP-i-tl): The city where the government of a country or a state is located

coast (kohst): The land next to the ocean or sea

emperor (EM-pr-ur): A ruler

peninsula (puh-NIN-suh-luh): A piece of land mostly surrounded by water but attached to a larger land area

territory (TEH-ruh-tor-ee): Any one of the large parts that some countries are divided into

tropical (TROP-ih-kuhl): Having hot, humid weather year round

Index

About the Author

Tracy Vonder Brink

Tracy Vonder Brink loves to visit new places. She has never visited India, but she enjoys Indian food. She lives in Cincinnati, Ohio, with her husband, two daughters, and two rescue dogs.

Written by: Tracy Vonder Brink
Designed by: Rhea Magaro
Series Development: James Earley
Proofreader: Melissa Boyce
Educational Consultant: Marie Lemke M.Ed.

Photographs: All images from Shutterstock

Crabtree Publishing

crabtreebooks.com 800-387-7650

Printed in the U.S.A./062024/CG20240201

Published in Canada
Crabtree Publishing
616 Welland Avenue
St. Catharines, Ontario
L2M 5V6

Published in the United States
Crabtree Publishing
347 Fifth Avenue
Suite 1402-145
New York, New York, 10016

Library and Archives Canada Cataloguing in Publication
Available at Library and Archives Canada

Library of Congress Cataloging-in-Publication Data
Available at the Library of Congress

Hardcover: 978-1-0398-4481-0
Paperback: 978-1-0398-4562-6
Ebook (pdf): 978-1-0398-4634-0
Epub: 978-1-0398-4704-0
Read-Along: 978-1-0398-4774-3
Audio: 978-1-0398-4844-3